A MASSIVE BOOK FULL OF FECKIN' IRISH SLANG THAT'S GREAT CRAIC FOR ANY SHOWER OF SAVAGES

Colin Murphy is a right head-the-ball. Fourteen years ago, he and Dosser O'Dea were on the batter, fluthered, when they decided to give book-writing a bit of a lash. About twenty books later he's still bashing out Feckin' books by the gansey-load, mostly to pay for more of the hard stuff so he can get rat-arsed again. He is married to a fine thing called Gráinne and they have two yokes of grown-up kids who are still costing them a wojus load of spondulics.

Donal O'Dea is a mentaller who's usually in rag order. He thinks he's Leonardo da Feckin' Vinci with his fierce illustrations, but he's really only a doss artist. He's been designing the Feckin' books for yonks now, that's when he's not banjaxing the advertising agency he works in. Somehow, a couple of decades ago he persuaded the deadly Karen to marry him and they have a load of snappers who are a right shower of savages.

A MASSIVE BOOK FULL OF FECKIN' IRISH SLANG THAT'S GREAT CRAIC FOR ANY SHOWER OF SAVAGES

Colin Murphy & Donal O'Dea

THE O'BRIEN PRESS
DUBLIN

First published 2016 by The O'Brien Press Ltd,
12 Terenure Road East, Rathgar, Dublin 6, D06 HD27, Ireland.
Tel: +353 I 4923333; Fax: +353 I 4922777
E-mail: books@obrien.ie
Website: www.obrien.ie
Includes material from *The Book of Feckin' Irish Slang That's Great Craic for
Cute Hoors and Bowsies* (2004) and *The 2nd Feckin' Book of Irish Slang That
Makes a Holy Show of the First One* (2006).
Reprinted 2018.
The O'Brien Press is a member of Publishing Ireland.

ISBN: 978-1-84717-871-8

2 4 6 8 9 7 5 3
18 20 22 21 19

Printed and bound in Poland by Białostockie Zakłady Graficzne S.A.
The paper in this book is produced using pulp from managed forests

Published in

DUBLIN

UNESCO
City of Literature

What's the story?

'Did you hear that the scrubber and the wagon were plastered last night and ended up in a mill? It was deadly!'

This sentence makes perfect sense to most Irish people. But to everyone else on the planet it means the following:

'Did you hear that the cleaning utensil and the four-wheeled, horse-drawn vehicle were covered in a lime/sand/water mixture and then transported to a processing factory, with fatal consequences?'

This newly compiled compendium sets out to avoid any such confusion arising in the future by explaining in clear and precise terms the meaning of a vast collection of commonly used Irish slang words or expressions. If you, dear reader, believe that any of the listed phrases have been incorrectly translated, please feel free to go and ask my arse.

Acting the maggot (expr)

Fooling about in a somewhat boisterous manner.

(usage) 'Anto! Will you stop acting de maggot and give the oul' wan back her wheelchair.'

Afters (n)

Dessert.

(usage) 'I had a batter burger and chips for the main course and a flagon of cider for afters.'

IT'S A COMBINATION LOCK.
THEY'RE CALLED THE BUST-PROOF BRA.

Ages (n)

A very long time
indeed.
*(usage) 'It took me ages
to get her bra open.'*

Alco (n)

Person who is
regularly inebriated.
*(usage) 'Just because
I've been injecting vodka
into my oranges doesn't
make me an alco.'*

Amadán (n)

Idiot. Imbecile. Fool.
*(usage) 'Yes, Your
Honour, I arrested
the amadán as he
attempted to burgle the
Garda station.'*

Animal (adj)

Superb. Very exciting.
*(usage) 'That time
we put the banger
up the cat's arse was
absolutely animal!'*

Any use? (expr)

Was it any good?
(usage) 'Is he any use in bed since he got dem Viagra on the internet?'

Apache (n)

A joyrider.
(usage) 'That smart-arsed little apache fecker calls himself "Dances with Porsches".'

RIGHT, MY LITTLE APACHE FECKER – PREPARE TO BE SCALPED!

Arra be whist (expr)

Be quiet. Shut up.
*(usage) 'Arra, be whist
worrying, doctor. Sure
haven't I cut down to
sixty fags a day?'*

Arseology (n)

Nonsense. Gibberish.
*(usage) 'If you ask me,
Jacintha's proctologist
talks a lot of arseology.'*

Arseways (adj)

Mishmash. Complete
disarray. Total mess.
*(usage) 'Me car has
been arseways since I
ran over the pedestrian.'*

Article (n)(derog)

> A person.
> *(usage) 'Our English
> teacher is a drunken
> old lech. In fact, he's a
> definite article.'*

Ask me arse (v)(rhetorical)

> What do you take me
> for, a silly billy?
> *(usage) 'Lend YOU a
> fiver? Go and ask me
> arse!'*

Atallatallatall (expr)

Emphatic 'in any way'.
(usage) 'Hey, Concepta!
Any chance of a ride
atallatallatall?'
'Go and ask me arse
me arse me arse.'

Babby (n)

Baby. Small child.
(usage) 'Me Ma had her
first babby when she
was fifteen. So I thought
I'd keep the family
tradition goin'.'

Bad dose (n)

Severe illness.
(usage) 'I'd a bad dose
of the scutters after
them ten pints of
Guinness last night.'

Bags (n)

A botched job.
*(usage) 'The hairdresser
made a right bags of
me perm.'*

Bang on (adj)

Correct. Perfectly
accurate.
*(usage) 'That shot ye
took at the ref's groin
was bang on.'*

Banjaxed (adj)

Broken. Severely damaged.
(usage) 'Me marriage to Deco is completely banjaxed.'

Barrel (v)

Hurry. Race. Rush.
(usage) 'When the Guards arrived, the Minister for Justice barrelled out of the lap dancing club.'

Beamer (n)

When one's face goes red with embarrassment.
(usage) 'I had a right beamer on me when me top came off in the pool.'

Begorrah (expr)

By God! (Note: Word does not exist outside Hollywood movies.)
(usage) American actor 1: 'Begorrah, me lad, 'tis a fine soft mornin' to be sure.'
American actor 2: "Tis, to be sure, to be sure, begorrah and bejapers.'
Irish actor: 'Excuse me while I throw up.'

Bejapers (expr)

By Jesus!
(usage) American actor 1: 'Bejapers, Mickeen, I've lost me shillelagh!'
American actor 2: 'Begorrah, Pat, maybe the fairies stole it.'
Irish actor: 'If you don't shut up I'm going to stab you in the eye with a pencil.'

Belt (n)(v)

A thump with the fist.
To strike.
*(usage) 'Me mot gave
me a belt just because
I told her I'd slept with
her Ma.'*

BIFFO (acronym)

Big Ignorant Fucker
from Offaly.
*(usage) 'Em, excuse me,
BIFFO, would you mind
not using the tablecloth
as a hanky?'*

Bits and bobs (expr)

An assortment of
random items or
actions.
*(usage) 'I'm planning
to tax various new bits
and bobs this year,
Taoiseach, like doors,
sex and air.'*

Black (adj)

Extremely crowded.
(usage) 'Deadly, Anto! This place is black with women. Funny name though, The Lesbar.'

Black Maria (n)

Garda van.
(usage) 'The Black Maria was full of planning officials.'

Black stuff (n)

Stout.
(usage) 'Nine pints of the black stuff and a gin and tonic for de mot, please.'

Blarney (n)

Nonsense talk used to charm foreigners.
(e.g.) *'They say the ghost of Finn Mac Cumhall still stalks the Grand Canal. Buy another round and I'll tell you all about it, my American friend.'*

Blather (n)(v)

Empty, worthless talk.
(usage) 'What are ye blatherin' on about now, President Higgins?'

BLATHER ...
BLATHER ...

B.L.O. (expr)

Be look-out. Keep
watch.
*(usage) 'Hey, Mick!
B.L.O. while I hook the
foreman's car bumper
to this crane.'*

RIGHT, POKER IT IS!
WHO'S GOING TO B.L.O
FOR THE TAOISEACH?

CABINET
ROOM

Bob, a few (expr)

An unspecified
amount of money.
*(usage) 'So the bank
executive stashed a
few bob in the Cayman
Islands?'*
'Yeah, €27 million.'

Bog (1) (n)

Rural Ireland.
(usage) Dub 1: 'Y'know, down de bog dey've never heard of curry chips.'
Dub 2: 'Jaysus. So dey're not sophisticated like us?'

Bog (2) (n)

The toilet.
(usage) 'Great. You might have told me your bog's out of order before you served me the vindaloo and seven lagers.'

Bogtrotter (n)

A person of rural extraction.

(usage) 'And that, my bogtrotter friend, is what we call electricity.'

Bold thing, the (expr)

Sexual intercourse.

(usage) 'Me Ma's always tellin' me not to be bold, and then I heard her tell her friend she'd done the bold thing with the milkman three times.'

Bollixed (adj)

Somewhat in excess
of the legal alcohol
driving limit.
*(usage) 'After twelve
pints I was a bit
bollixed.'*

Bowsie (n)

Person (esp. male)
of very disreputable
character. A useless
good-for-nothing.
*(usage) 'Is there anyone
in the Government who
isn't a bleedin' bowsie?'*

Boyo (n)

Male juvenile (esp. delinquent).
(usage) 'Y'know, sarge, I think dem boyos outside the off-licence are up to no good with dem crowbars and flick-knives.'

Brasser (n)

A lady of the night.
(usage) 'As a judge, it's my job to keep brassers like you off the street. So get into the bloody car!'

Brickin' it (v)

Extremely nervous or scared.
(usage) 'I've been brickin' it ever since I used her green party dress to make a flag for the Ireland match.'

Brutal (adj)

Awful, terrible, hideous.
(usage) 'The head on her was brutal.'

Bucketing down (v)

Raining cats and dogs.
(usage) 'Sure it's bucketing down outside. Might as well have another six pints.'

Bucko (n)(derog)

Unsavoury or untrustworthy youth. *(usage) Garda: 'Y'know sarge, I suspect that fella standing on that poor oul' wan's head is a bit of a bucko.'*

Business, The (n)

Something cool. *(usage) 'The sporty lights on me new car are the business!'*

NOW THAT'S WHAT I CALL THE BUSINESS!

THE SEE-THRU LINGERIE COMPANY

Caboosh, the whole (expr)

Everything or everyone.
(usage) 'The whole caboosh of bankers got big fat pensions.'

Cacks (n)

Underwear (esp. male).
(usage) 'Me boyfriend changes his cacks so little that he doesn't have to drop them, he just hits them and they shatter.'

Cat (adj)

Terrible. Useless.
(usage) 'My guard dog is cat.'

MEOW

Caught rapid (expr)

Caught in the act.
Proven guilty beyond
doubt.
*(usage) 'I was caught
rapid in bed with me
mistress by me bit on
the side.'*

Chancer (n)

Untrustworthy
person.
*(usage) 'The Minister
for Justice is a right
chancer.'*

Chance your arm (expr)

Give something a try,
take a gamble.
*(usage) 'I'll chance me
arm de wife won't be
able to smell de tenth
pint.'*

Chiseller (n)

Young child.
(usage) 'That slapper's only eighteen and she's already had three chisellers.

Clatter (v)(n)

To slap playfully with palm.
(usage) 'I only gave him one little clatter, yer Honour. His skull musta been brittle.'

Cod (v)

To pull one's leg in a
jovial fashion.
*(usage) 'Ah, sure I was
only coddin'. Your wife
wasn't electrocuted at
all.'*

Codology (n)

Nonsense, foolish
talk, lies.
*(usage) 'The minister's
expenses claim is a load
of codology.'*

Cog (v)

To illicitly copy
someone else's work
(esp. at school).
*(usage) 'Basically I
cogged all my exam
papers. That's how I
became a teacher.'*

Coola boola (expr)

I understand.
Excellent!
(usage) 'Ye want me te stamp on the goalie's head, boss? Coola boola!'

Cop on (v)

Get wise. Don't be so stupid.
(usage) 'Me wife really needs to cop on – she got angry just cause I wanted a threesome with her and her sister.'

AH GET A BIT OF COP ON, YE MANKY WAGON!

GO AND ASK ME ARSE, YE GANKY MUCK SAVAGE.

Craic (n)

(Pronounced crack)

Fun.

(usage) 'There's great craic to be found in that pub on the corner.'

(Note: Misinterpretation of this expression has led to several arrests of foreign visitors who were caught trying to purchase a particular illicit drug.)

Culchie (n)

A person whose birthplace is beyond Dublin city limits.

(usage) Q: 'What d'ye call a culchie in a stretch Limo?'

A: 'The deceased.'

Cute hoor (n)

Suspiciously resourceful gentleman. *(usage) 'Speaking from his yacht off Bermuda, the cute hoor denied he'd made any payments to politicians in return for favourable building contracts.'*

Da (n)

Father. Dad. *(usage) 'According to me Ma, me Da was someone called "bollixhead".'*

Dander (n)

Lazy stroll. *(usage) 'Hey Mary, can we hurry this dander to the pub up a bit?'*

Deadly (adj)

Great, brilliant, fantastic.
(usage) *'Yer woman's got a deadly arse.'*

HE WAS DISTRACTED BY A GIRL'S ARSE AND DROVE OVER A CLIFF.

NOW THAT'S WHAT I CALL DEADLY!

Deadner (n)

To punch someone sharply at the top of the arm.
(usage) *'Hey Damo, let's give that guy with his arm in a sling a deadner!'*

Dekko (n)

A look at. An inspection.
(usage) 'Jaysus! Have a dekko at the shape of yer woman's arse!'

YEAH, I'LL BE RIGHT THERE, MARY. I'M JUST HAVING A DEKKO AT THE LOCAL, EH, WILDLIFE.

Dense (adj)

Stupid. Thick.
(usage) 'My accountant and solicitor say that paying tax is dense.'

Desperate (adj)

(Pronounced despera) Dreadful, awful.
(usage) 'Yer man's arse is desperate after a few pints.'

Diddies (n)

Extremely childish term for a woman's breasts.
(usage) 'Counsel for the defence has got a magnificent pair of diddies, hasn't she, m'Lud?'

Diddle (v)

Cheat. Swindle.
(usage) 'Madame Esmerelda foretold that I was going to be diddled, then charged me €130.'

Diddly-eye/diddly-i (adj)

Term describing Irish music (may be offensive to traditional musicians).
(usage) 'The tourists love a bit of the oul' diddly-eye music.'

... DO BE DO BE DOOOO

Do be/does be (expr)

Grammatically incorrect use of present continuous tense.
(usage) 'Hey Mick, I do be listening to that Frank Sinatra in the car. You know the one? Do be do be doooo ...'

Dog's bollocks, the (expr)

First-rate. Perfect. Genuine.
(usage) 'That gobshite with the Rottweiler thinks he's the dog's bollox.'

Doing a line (expr)

Courting. Going out steadily with someone.
(usage) 'So I asked her if she fancied doing a line with me, and she tells me to feck off and get my own cocaine.'

Donkey's years (n)

AIRPORT RAIL LINK
Officially opened
2098 A.D.

Inordinately long time. An epoch. Time immemorial.
(e.g.) Period of time people of Ireland have been waiting for an airport rail link.

Don't be talkin' (expr)

You're right about
that. Don't remind
me.
*(usage) Mary:'Biddy,
do you think I'm a big-
mouth?'*
Biddy:'Don't be talkin'.'

Dosh (n)

Money.
*(usage) 'The lawyers in
those tribunals get an
awful lot of dosh.'*

DOSS ARTIST UNKNOWN

Doss artist (n)

Layabout who draws
the dole despite
availability of work.
*(usage) 'My husband
used to do the odd bit
of painting. Now he's
just a doss artist.'*

Dosser (n)

Lazy person.
*(usage) 'If they gave
out awards for being a
dosser, Mick would be
too lazy to go up and
collect the bleedin thing.'*

Doss, on the (n)

Failure to attend
school/work during
specified hours.
*'I swear I wasn't on de
doss. I really did have
leukaemia yesterday.'*

Doxie (n)

Dockland prostitute.
*(usage) 'The legs on
that doxie, Shay ...
I think me ship's just
come in!'*

Drawers (n)

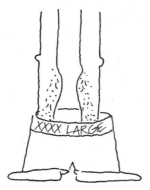

Knickers. Panties.
*(usage) 'You could fit a
hurling team into me
wife's drawers. In fact
I think she does on a
regular basis.'*

Dry shite (n)

Someone of limited verbal/social skills. *(usage) 'There was a dry shite on the seat beside me at the client party.'*

Dub (n)

Dubliner. *(usage) 'Did you know, Mick, that the Dubs have an annual award for the person who litters the most?'*

Eat the head off (v)

To rebuke verbally in an aggressive manner. *(usage) 'The missus ate the head off me just because I puked into de back of the TV.'*

Eccer (n)

Homework.
*(usage) 'Hey, Ma. Do
me eccer for me or
I'll tell Da about the
postman.'*

Edgemecation (n)

Ironic term for
education, implying
the subject doesn't
have any.
*(usage) 'The only sex
edgemecation I ever
got was behind the bike
shed.'*

Eejit (n)

Person of limited mental
capacity. Incapable
fool. Complete moron.
Imbecile.
*(e.g.) Person(s) responsible
for Ireland's health service.*

Effin' and blindin' (expr)

Swearing profusely.
*(usage) 'The Taoiseach was
effin' and blindin' because
the new Government jet
didn't have the Playboy
Channel.'*

Eff off (v)

Restrained/polite swear word used in refined Irish society. *(usage) 'Father, those chappies on the factory floor told me to "eff off" when I inquired if they'd made my morning tea.'*

Elephants (adj)

Extremely drunk. *(usage) 'Those two old cows at the bar are elephants.'*

Fag (n)

Cigarette.
*(usage) 'Aaah, Jaysus,
Trish. I know I'm not
that good in bed, but
couldn't you wait until
I'm finished before you
have your fag?'*

Fair play! (expr)

Well done!
*(usage) 'Fair play te ye
for gettin' de leg over
Deirdre.'*

Fanny (n)

Female genitals.
(usage) 'That Deirdre's fanny was as tight as a camel's hole in a sandstorm.'
(Warning: Some American visitors have inadvertently caused shock or offence through the mistaken belief that 'fanny' refers to buttocks, as it does in the US. For example, 'After that bike ride, I feel like giving my fanny a good rub,' may raise some eyebrows if spoken aloud in Ireland.)

OH FECK, I SAID F**K!!!

Feck (v)(n)

Politically correct term for f**k.
(usage) 'Ah feck off, Father Murphy. You're nothing but a feckin' fecker.'

Few scoops (expr)

A few drinks.
*(usage) Joe: 'Fancy a
few scoops before the
match?'*
*Tony: 'Deffo. It'll
probably improve me
game.'*

Fierce (adj)

Very. Extremely.
*(usage) 'I had a fierce
bad headache after
drinking Deirdre's
perfume.'*

Fine thing (n)

An attractive man or woman.

(usage) 'She looks like a fine thing after seven pints.'

Fire away (v)

Go ahead. Please commence.

(usage) 'So he asks me for a look at my shotgun, and I told the gobshite to fire away!'

Fit to be tied (expr)

Very angry.
(usage) 'I was fit to be tied when Deco suggested we try bondage.'

Flahulach (adj)

(Pronounced flah-hule-uck)

Generous.
(usage) 'The councillor was feeling flahulach after he got his bribe from the property developer.'

Flaming (adj)

Extremely drunk.
(usage) 'She was so flamin' she went out like a light.'

Fleece (v)

To rip off.
(usage) 'She was fleeced at the sheep market.'

I THOUGHT IT WAS A POODLE.

Flicks (plural n)

The movies. The cinema.
(usage) 'Seamo took me to see Deep Throat *in the flicks. He said it was a movie about a giraffe.'*

Flute (n)

Male sexual organ.
(usage) 'My boyfriend doesn't so much have a flute as a tin whistle.'

Fluthered (adj)

Having a high blood/ alcohol ratio.
(usage) 'I was so fluthered last night I slept with the missus.'

Fooster (v)

Not getting much done. Fiddling about. *(usage) 'Will ye stop foosterin' about, Mick, and stamp on the goalie's face!'*

Full shilling, not the (adj)

Mentally challenged. Not fully sane. Nuts. *(e.g.) Anyone who attempts to commute by means of public transport in Dublin or Cork on a regular basis is said to be 'not the full shilling'.*

Gaa (n)

Sport played by
the G.A.A. (Gaelic
Athletic Association).
*(usage) 'Gaa is a great
game. It's just a shame
about the G.A.A.'*

GAA HEADQUARTERS

NO FOREIGN SPORTS
ALLOWED
(EXCEPT AMERICAN
FOOTBALL, WHICH BRINGS
IN LOADSA WONGA).

Gaff (n)

Home. Place of
residence.
*(usage) 'Dat's some gaff
yer man de President
has in de Phoenix Park.'*

Gameball (expr)

Great. Excellent. I
agree. Ok.
*(usage) 'At the end of
camogie matches, the
girls are going to swap
their shirts? Gameball!'*

Gammy (adj)

Damaged. Crooked.
Useless.
*(usage) 'The entire
Cabinet is gammy.'*

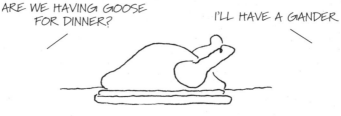

Gander (n)

A quick glance.
*(usage) 'I'd give anything
for a gander at Noleen
in the nip.'*

Ganky (adj)

Repulsive. Ugly.
*(usage) Q. What's the
difference between a
ganky-looking girl and
an absolute ride?
A. About ten pints!*

Gansey (n)

Jumper. Sweater.
Pullover.
*(usage) 'I'd love to be
inside her gansey on a
cold day like this.'*

Gansey-load (adj)

Many. Lots. An
excess.
*(usage) 'There's a
gansey-load of dossers
in the Dáil.'*

NOW THAT'S
WHAT I CALL A
GANSEY-LOAD!

Gargle (n)(v)

Drink (alcohol).
(usage) 'The Cabinet single-handedly prevented the closure of the brewery by retiring to the Dáil bar for a "gargle or two".'

Gas (adj)

Amusing. Funny. Hilarious.
(usage) 'It was gas when Cormac broke his collar-bone.'

Gawk (v)

To stare rudely.
(usage) 'What are you gawking at, ye ignorant gobshite?'

Gee (n)

Female reproductive organ.
(usage) 'I've a pain in me gee trying to get laid tonight.'

Geebag (n)

Woman of unpleasant character.
(usage) 'Me wife's a right geebag.'

Gee-eyed (adj)

Having partaken of a
large quantity of ales/
spirits.
*(orig) Subject is so
inebriated that his
eyes have shifted from
the normal horizontal
orientation.*

Gerrup-de-yard (expr)

Get lost!
*(usage) 'Wha', €12 for
a vodka and orange?
Gerrup-de-yard!'*

Get off with (v)

Be successful with a
romantic advance.
*(usage) 'I got off with
four different fellas at
the Christmas party.'*

Gift (adj)

Expression of pleasant
surprise.
*(usage) 'So they're going
to put all of Ireland's
estate agents in a
ship and sink it in the
Atlantic? Gift!'*

Gingernut (n)

Redheaded man or woman.
(usage) 'I've always wondered, Edna, do gingernuts like you just have red hair on your head or ... Ow! Jaysus, me eye!'

Git (n)

Contemptible male.
(usage) 'You stupid git! You puked in me pocket!'

OUR NEW APPRENTICES WILL BE KNOWN AS GENERAL INSURANCE TRAINEES. OR G.I.T.S FOR SHORT

IRISH INSURANCE LTD.

Give out (v)

Nag or criticise someone.

(usage) 'The minister finally gave out to the British government after Sellafield exploded and wiped out the east coast of Ireland.'

Go (n)

A fight.

(usage) 'Yes, Your Honour, I did have a go at him. Then Knuckler had a go, then Mauler had a go, then Crusher Molloy had a go, then ...'

Go and shite! (expr)

I am not in agreement with your suggestion.

(usage) 'The priest told me to abstain from bad language, so I told him to go and shite!'

Gob (1) (n)

Mouth.
(usage) 'I wish the Minister for Justice would keep his gob shut.'

Gob (2) (v)

To expectorate forcefully.
(usage) 'So I hear you gobbed the PE teacher in the ear, headmaster?'

THAT'S WHAT I CALL THE 'GOB' OF THE SEASON

Gobdaw (n)

Person of restricted mental ability.
(usage) 'The Minister for Finance is a complete gobdaw.'

Gobshite (n)

Person of below-average IQ. Socially inept individual.
(usage) 'The Minister for Finance is a complete gobshite.'

Gollier (n)

A mass of phlegm expelled from mouth at high speed.
(usage) 'I landed a gollier in the geography teacher's coffee.'

Gombeen man (n)

WHATEVER YOU SAY, MINISTER

Petty, snivelling, fawning underling. *(e.g.) Chief executive of any Irish semi-state company.*

Gossoon (n)

Small child. *(usage) 'I'll have to stop leaving me little gossoon with me husband. His first words were: "Jaysus, I've a pain in me bollox."'*

Gouger (n)

Aggressive, repulsive person. *(usage) 'Do you really take this gouger to be your lawful wedded husband?'*

Gowanouddadat!/ Gowayouddadat! (expr)

You're pulling my leg.
You're exaggerating.
*(usage) 'You're a
fan of Bertie Ahern?
Gowanouddadat!'*

Grand (adj)

Good. Fine.
*(usage) Government
Minister: 'Ripping off
people is grand with us!'*

Guff (n)

Feeble excuses.
Blatant lies.
*(e.g.) 'Sorry I'm late,
boss. I had to take me
Ma to the hospital for
her spine replacement
operation.'*

Gullier (n)

In the game of
marbles, the largest.
*(usage) 'Hey, mister, can
I borrow your glass eye
to use as a gullier?'*

Gummin' (v)

Dying for. Can't wait
for.
*(usage) 'Yer wan with
the false teeth is
gummin' for a snog.'*

Gurrier (n)

Hooligan. Delinquent.
Ruffian.
*(usage) 'Give the oul' lad
back his teeth, ye little
gurrier!'*

Hames (n)

Complete mess.
*(usage) 'The plastic
surgeon made
a hames of me
arse.'*

Ha'penny place (expr)

I DON'T CARE WHERE
YOU LIVE. I NEED TO
SPEND A PENNY.

A lowly position
or status.
*(usage) 'You want to
see the kip we're livin'
in, Deirdre — even the
address is 13 Ha'penny
Place!'*

Hardchaw (n)

Tough guy, easily
provoked.
*(usage) 'He's such a
hardchaw he opens his
beer bottles with his
nostril.'*

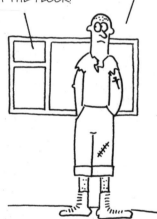

I DON'T CARE WHO
YOU HAVE TO BEAT
UP. GET IN HERE AND
WASH THE FLOOR!

YES, MA.

Hash (n)

Mess. Foul-up.
*(usage) 'He made a
hash of rolling the hash.'*

Head-the-ball (n)

Term of address:
'you'.
(usage) 'Hey, head-the-ball, how do I get to Donegal?'

HEY, HEAD-THE-BALL!!!
KICK IT!!!

Heavin' (adj)

Thoroughly packed.
(usage) 'In the planning trial, the defendant's box was heavin' with County Councillors.'

Heifer (n)

A very unattractive girl.

(usage) 'She may be a feckin' heifer, but she's got a great set of udders.'

AND DO YOU, MICK, TAKE THIS HEIFER ... SORRY ... HEATHER TO BE YOUR LAWFUL WEDDED ...

Herself/It's herself (n/term of address)

The woman of the hour. The boss. The wife or partner.

(usage) 'Oh, shite. Here comes herself with a right puss on her.'

Hidin' (n)

A beating. A heavy
defeat in sport.
*(usage) 'We gave the
opposition a right hidin'
but still lost 6-0.'*

Himself/It's himself (n/term of address)

The man of the
hour. The boss. The
husband or partner.
*(usage) 'Himself was
so rat-arsed last night
he peed into the sugar
bowl.'*

Hockeyed (v)

Heavily defeated.
(usage) 'Ireland hockeyed Brazil five-nil in the World Cup final, and then me bleedin' missus woke me up.'

Hole (n)

Anus.
(usage) 'Piles are a pain in the hole.'

Holliers (n)

Holidays. Vacation.
(usage) Girl 1: 'So I hear you and Mick never left your room your entire holliers …?' (giggle) Girl 2: 'Yeah. The gobshite was langered for two weeks.'

Holy Joe (n)

Self-righteous, sanctimonious hypocrite.
(usage) 'If Holy Joes are so holy, how come there's always so many of them queuing for confession?'

PLEASE GOD, CAN THERE
BE WORLD PEACE AND CAN
I HAVE A NEW CAR?

Holy show (expr)

Disgrace. Spectacle.
(usage) 'Me Ma made a holy show of herself when she dropped her pint into the baptismal font.'

Hoof (1) (v)

To walk hurriedly.
*(usage) 'The judge
hoofed it out of the
massage parlour when
the Guards arrived.'*

Hoof (2) (v)

To kick a ball very
hard and high.
*(usage) 'He's great at
hoofing the ball over the
bar. Just a shame we're
playing soccer.'*

Hooley (n)

Raucous celebration involving drinking and singing.
(usage) '... and folks, I'm asked to invite you all to a hooley in Murphy's pub immediately after Mick's funeral.'

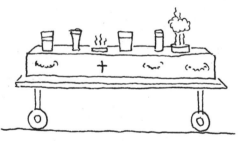

Hop (v)

FANCY GOIN' ON THE HOP?

Play truant from school.
(usage) 'Let's go on the hop and get pissed. I'm fed up teaching those bleedin' kids anyway.'

JAYSUS, I'M REALLY IN THE HORRORS AFTER LAST NIGHT.

YE OLD HANGOVER CURE

Horrors (n)

Bad hangover.
(usage) 'I'm really in the horrors this morning. I think that fifteenth pint must have been bad.'

Howaya (greeting)

Hello. Hi.
(usage) 'Howaya, ye big bollix!'

How's she cuttin'? (expr)

How is life, my good friend?
(usage) 'How's she cuttin', Yer Honour?'

How's the craic? (expr)

How are you? What's
happening?
*(usage) 'How's the craic,
Deirdre?'*

Hump, the (n)

In a sulk.
*(usage) 'He got the
hump 'cause I wouldn't
give him a hump.'*

Hunkers, on your (expr)

Squatting.
*(usage) 'Hey Mick, if
you get on your hunkers
like this you can see up
yer wan's skirt!'*

I will in me arse/ bollix/hole/fanny (expr)

I absolutely refuse to
do what you suggest.
*(usage) 'Marry you? I
will in me bollix!'*

I won't, no (expr)

I will, yes.
*(usage) 'One for the
road? I won't, no.'*

Jack (n)

Dubliner.
*(usage) 'Tradesmen
in Dublin are so shite
they're called Jacks of
all trades.'*

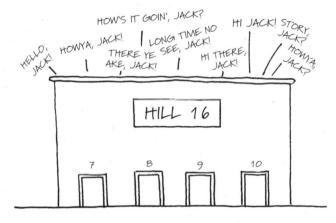

Jacked (adj)

Exhausted.
*(usage) Solicitor: 'I'm
jacked from counting all
the money I've made
from tribunals.'*

Jackeen (n)

A rural person's
derogatory name for
a Dubliner.
*(usage) Q: 'What does a
Jackeen say on his first
day in work?'
A: 'What do I do now,
Daddy?'*

Jack-in-the-box (n)

Dead Dubliner.
*(usage) 'Here lies a
jack-in-the-box. He lived,
he littered, he died.'*

Jacks (n)

Toilet, restroom.
*(usage) 'Ye tink dat's bad?
Wait 'til ye see de state
of de jacks in de Dáil.'*

DÁIL
TOILETS

I WOULDN'T GO
IN THERE. THE
MINISTER'S GOT
VERBAL DIARRHOEA.

Jaded (adj)

Very tired.
*(usage) Biddy: 'You look
jaded. Did you sleep with
Mick?'
Clare: 'Well, we didn't
exactly do much
sleeping.'*

Jammers (adj)

Extremely crowded.
(usage) 'The Dáil bar is permanently jammers.'

Jammy (adj)

Exceedingly lucky.
(usage) 'The jammy bastard won the Lotto again.'

Janey Mack! (expr)

Expression of utter disbelief. Wow!
(usage) 'Janey Mack! That politician told the truth!'

Japers (expr)

Wow!
*(usage) Nurse 1:'Japers,
sister, the suppository
for that man was very
big!'
Nurse 2:'Hey, has
anyone seen my
thermos?'*

Jar (n)

Pint of beer or stout.
*(usage) 'I'm dying for
a jar. The court will
adjourn until 2pm.'*

Jarred (adj)

Having consumed
excess alcohol.
*(usage) 'It only takes
one drink to get her
jarred. The twelfth.'*

Jaysus! (expr)

Jesus Christ!
(usage) 'Ah Jaysus, ye puked in me pint!'

Joe Soap (n)

Anybody. Somebody.
Nondescript person.
(usage) 'I shagged some Joe Soap last night.'

WHAT ARE YOU GOING TO CALL HIM, MRS SOAP?

JOE!

Jo Maxi (n)

Taxi. Cab.
(usage) 'Eh, hello. I'd like a Jo Maxi please to collect four people from Madame Le Whip's Maison de Plaisir and take us back to Government Buildings.'

Kick the shite out of (v)

Violently assault, causing actual bodily harm.
(usage) 'Right, lads, we're down 2-0. Let's kick the shite out of dem.'

Kilt (expr)

In some discomfort. In serious trouble, as in 'killed'.
(usage) 'I'm kilt listening to party political broadcasts.'

HERE LIES
COLIN MURPHY –
KILT LISTENING
TO POLITICIANS

Kip (n)

A place/establishment of poor repute. A dump.
(usage) 'Benidorm is a kip.'

Kithogue (n)

Left-handed or clumsy person.
(usage) 'He's a real kithogue in bed.'

Knackered (adj)

Extremely tired.
(usage) Supermarket MD: 'I'll never get knackered ripping Irish people off.'

Knick-knacking (expr)

Ringing a doorbell and
then hiding.
*(usage) 'The British
Ambassador was caught
knick-knacking at the
French Embassy.'*

SO YOU'VE FINALLY
HAD THE JOB DONE
ON YOUR KNOCKERS

YEAH, I HAD
THEM REDUCED

Knockers (n)

Mammaries. Breasts.
*(usage) 'Are dem
knockers real, missus?'*

Lady Muck (n)

Self-important, stuck-up woman.
(usage) 'She's a right Lady Muck, havin' a gin and tonic with her chips!'

LADIES AND GENTLEMEN, THE RIGHT HONOURABLE LORD AND LADY MUCK.

Lamp out of (v)

To hit someone very hard.
(usage) Garda: 'Well, the guy was marching for world peace, so naturally I lamped him out of it.'

Langer (n)

Male reproductive
organ.
*(usage) Countrywoman A:
'This carrot reminds me
of me husband's langer.'
Countrywoman B: 'Ye
mean the size of it?'
Countrywoman A: 'No.
The dirt of it.'*

Langered (adj)

Very drunk.
(usage) 'I was so langered I woke up with a kebab in me knickers.'

Lash (v)

To rain heavily.
(usage) 'We had two weeks' holiday in the sunny south-east and it never stopped bleedin' lashin'.'

Lash, give a (expr)

Attempt. Try against the odds.
(usage) 'She asked me if I wanted to try BDSM so I said I'd give it a lash.'

Legger (n)

A rapid exit from a situation.
(usage) 'The milkman had to do a legger when me husband came home.'

Leg it (v)

To flee rapidly. To run away.
(usage) 'Let's leg it before the waiter comes back with the bill, Sarge.'

Legless (adj)

So drunk one can't
stand.
*(usage) 'I asked Pat
to get something that
would make me look
sexy. So he went out
and got legless.'*

I GOT LEGLESS
LAST NIGHT.

Let on (v)

To pretend.
(usage) '[Chuckling to himself] … No, you don't have a brain tumour, Mr Hogan, I was only letting on.'

HE SAID HE WAS GOING TO GET HIS PENIS ENLARGED, BUT I'M SURE HE WAS ONLY LETTING ON.

Life of Reilly (expr)

Living a carefree existence.
(usage) 'Being responsible for Ireland's health service is the life of Reilly!'

Loaf (v)

To head-butt.
*(usage) 'Righ', Murphy.
As a bouncer, your
primary job is to loaf
everyone who tries to
get into this bleedin'
nightclub.'*

Locked (adj)

In a state of total
inebriation.
*(usage) 'I was locked in
the pub all night.'*

Lookit (expr)

Listen to me! Hang on
a moment!
*(usage) 'Lookit, ref. The
centre forward's leg was
already broken before I
tackled him.'*

Loopers (adj)

Crazy.
(usage) *'It's loopers what psychiatrists charge.'*

Lose the head (v)

Lose one's temper.
(usage) *'She kicked him in the face and he lost the head.'*

Ma (n)

Mother.
(usage) 'His Ma has always spoiled him. She brought him his birthday cake in bed and managed to light all thirty-six candles.'

Mala (n)

Plasticine.
(usage) 'Look, Miss, I made my mala into the shape of me wil ... Ow!'

Manky (adj)

Disgustingly filthy.
(e.g.) Any street, waterway, public toilet, or beauty spot in Ireland.

WELCOME TO DUBLIN
Europe's mankiest city

Massive (adj)

Great. Fantastic.
*(usage) 'Look at the tiny
little arse on yer woman.
It's massive!'*

Mentaller (n)

Nut case. Looney.
*(usage) Politician:
'Commissioner, about
1,000 of the Gardai are
complete mentallers!'
Commissioner: 'I know.
It's just not enough, is it?'*

GARDA

NAME: KELLY
RANK: MENTALLER

Me oul' flower (expr)

> My darling.
> (usage) 'It's so good to
> see you again, Gráinne,
> me oul' flower.'
> 'I'm Carol.'

Merciful hour! (expr)

> Old-fashioned
> exclamation of shock.
> (usage) 'Merciful hour,
> Granny! Are you reading
> Fifty Shades of Grey?'

Messages (n)

Shopping.
(usage) 'I need to get a few messages – beer, stout, whiskey and five packs of fags.'

Mess, to (v)

To fool about.
(usage) 'I wasn't messin', Angela. I really do want to get your bra off.'

THEY'RE A PAIR OF MESSERS, ALL RIGHT.

MESSRS MORAN + HOGAN, SOLICITORS

Mickey (n)

Childish name for male organ.
(usage) 'When he sees a short skirt, his mickey's like a divining rod.'

Mighty (adj)

Brilliant. First rate.
(usage) 'Your new boobs are mighty, Deirdre!'

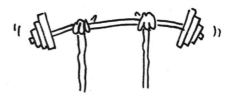

Mill (n)(v)

Fight. Public brawl.
(usage) 'Hey look, lads! A mill between wimmin'!'

THIS FOIS GRAS
BEATS CHIPS ANY DAY

Mill into (v)

Take to
enthusiastically.
*(usage) 'I always mill
into a cod and curry
chips after I get rat-
arsed.'*

Mind your house! (expr)

VROOM,
VROOM!

In team sports, a
warning of a tackle
from behind.
*(usage) 'Mind your
house, Anto! There's a
bleedin' bulldozer about
to demolish it!'*

DON'T WORRY, BARMAN. OF COURSE WE'RE OVER 18!

Mitch (v)

To play truant. To skip school.
(usage) 'Honest, we're not mitchin', Guard. We're doin' a project on juvenile alcohol consumption.'

Mortaller (n)

A mortal sin.
(usage) 'The price of car insurance in Ireland is a mortaller.'

COURSE IT'S NOT A MORTALLER, DEIRDRE. SURE I'D KNOW. I'M A BISHOP.

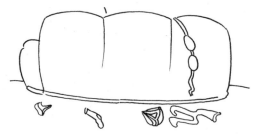

Mortified (adj)

Highly embarrassed.
*(usage) 'I was mortified
when the baby came
out black.'*

Mot (n)

Girlfriend.
*(usage) 'Me mot drinks
tequila sunrises like
there's no tomorrow.'*

Moxie/moxy (adj)

Very poor quality.
Lousy.
*(usage) 'The Irish health
service is the moxiest
on the planet.'*

Moxy-load (n)

A very large amount.
*(usage) Lawyer:'I made
a moxy-load of money
working at the tribunal!'*

Muck savage (n)

Country fellow lacking
in sophistication.
*(usage) 'No, you big
muck savage, you may
not eat curry chips in
the delivery room.'*

Mulchie (n)

Person from a small rural town.

(usage) 'That, my mulchie friend, is a three-storey building.'

BE THE HOKEY, WOULDYA
LOOK AT THE SIZE OF THAT.

Murder (adj)

Very difficult. Almost impossible.

(usage) 'Getting a Cavan man to buy his round is murder.'

Next nor near (expr)

Very near to.
(usage) 'I couldn't get next nor near the Dáil bar.'

Nifty (adj)

Extremely useful.
(usage) 'The current Government is the polar opposite of nifty.'

Nip, in the (adj)

Nude. Naked.
(usage) 'The doctor examined me in the nip. Whatever happened to his clothes is anyone's guess.'

Nippy (1) (adj)

Cold.
(usage) 'Her arse must
be a bit nippy wearing
that skirt.'

I'M SURE I CAN FEEL A DRAUGHT
FROM SOMEWHERE

Nippy (2) (adj)

Fast. Agile.
(usage) 'Her arse must
be a bit nippy wearing
that skirt.'

Nixer (n)

Job done on the side, for cash, thus avoiding tax.

(usage) 'Tell you what, I'll write your next Budget speech as a nixer, Minister.'

Noggin (n)

Head.

(usage) 'They say she gives great noggin.'

Not give a shite (expr)

Not give a damn.

(usage) 'The doctor didn't give a shite that I was constipated.'

Off one's face (expr)

YEP. I THINK I'M OFF ME FACE

Very drunk.
(usage) 'I was so off my face that I landed on my face.'

Oirish (n)

Mythical language and culture used by Americans and British when portraying Irish people.
(e.g.) 'Top of de mornin' te ye, be de hokey. D'ye happen te know, me good sir, where I'd be findin' a leprechaun dis fine day, at all at all?'

One and one (expr)

> Cod and chips.
> *(usage) 'Two one and ones, Dario.'*

On the batter (expr)

> Out getting drunk.
> *(usage) 'Please excuse my condition, I was on the batter last night. Now, please rise for the Lord's Prayer.'*

On the hop (expr)

> Playing truant. Absent without leave.
> *(usage) 'That bleedin' financier who ripped off the pension fund is on the hop in Brazil.'*

On the lash (expr)

A prolonged drinking session.

(usage) Solicitor: 'I ripped off so many people this week I could go on the lash for the rest of my natural life.'

On the piss (expr)

A prolonged drinking session.

(usage) 'I'm sick of this Dáil debate on the health service. Let's go on the piss, Minister.'

SORRY, SPUD. I CAN'T GO ON THE LASH TONIGHT. I'M GOING ON THE PISS WITH GRAINNE INSTEAD.

On the tear (expr)

A prolonged drinking session.
(usage) 'The County Councillors denied they'd been constantly on the tear during their fact-finding trip to Crete.'

Ossified (adj)

Totally inebriated.
(usage) 'Do you know it takes just three pints to get an Englishman ossified?'

THREE PINTS OF GUINNESS AND A SICK BUCKET FOR MY ENGLISH FRIEND.

Oul' fella (n)

Father.
(usage) 'Me oul' fella got me Ma pregnant when she was sixteen ...'

Oul' wan (n)

Mother.
(usage) '... and me oul' wan hasn't seen the bowsie since!'

Pain in the hole (expr)

THIS NEW RECTAL PROBE IS DESIGNED TO CURE PAINS IN THE HOLE.

Someone or something very irritating.
(usage) 'People from Dublin 4 are a pain in the hole.'

Paralytic (adj)

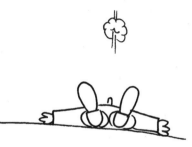

So inebriated one actually passes out.
(usage) 'Do you know that it takes just four pints to get an Englishman paralytic?'

Pelting (adj)

Raining heavily.
*(usage) 'The weather
forecast said sunny
weather, so it's bound to
be pelting.'*

Perishing (adj)

Extremely cold.
*(usage) 'Me and Anto
were perishin' havin' sex
under the bus shelter.'*

Petrified drunk (adj)

Completely
intoxicated.
*(usage) 'Y'know, Trish,
it's ironic that when he's
petrified drunk there's
one part of him that
never goes stiff.'*

Pick, not a (expr)

Skinny.
*(usage) 'Have another
helping, son, there's not
a pick on ye.'*
*'Ma, I'm twenty-two
stone.'*

Pile of shite (expr)

Something utterly
useless or terrible.
*(usage) 'The manure I
had delivered was a pile
of shite.'*

Piss up (n)

Night of revelry and imbibing alcohol.
(usage) 'I must interrupt counsel's lengthy summation to remind him that the barristers' annual piss-up starts at five.'

Plámás (n)(v)

Gaelic word for flattery.
(usage) 'Paddy Kelly tried to plámás me bra off.'

Plankin' it (v)

To be extremely nervous or scared.
(usage) 'She's been plankin' it ever since Mick's Celtic shirt came out of the wash dark blue.'

Plastered (adj)

Very drunk.
*(usage) 'I was so
plastered that the taxi
driver actually made
sense.'*

Póg (n)

Kiss.
*(usage) 'Well, it started
off as a little póg on
the cheek. I'm due in
September.'*

Powerful (adj)

Brilliant. Fantastic.
(usage) 'The power
in Robbo's new car is
powerful.'

Poxy (adj)

Terrible. Lousy.
(usage) 'What's the
condition of my rash,
doctor?'
'Poxy.'

LOVELY, SOFT, POXY DAY IN IRELAND

Proper order! (expr)

And rightly so! As it should be!

(usage) 'I hear they finally put a corrupt banker in jail.'

'Proper order!'

Puck (n)

Punch.

(usage) 'My dentist ripped me off so much I gave him a puck in the teeth.'

Puss (n)

Sulky face.
(usage) 'Frank had a puss on him just because me and the girls were watching Emmerdale *during the World Cup Final.'*

Quare (1) (adj)

Odd.
(usage) 'Isn't it a quare thing how car insurance in Ireland is ten times more expensive than everywhere else on the planet?'

IT'S VERY QUARE HOW WOMEN NEVER FOUND ME ATTRACTIVE BEFORE I WON THE LOTTO ...

Quare (2) (adj)

Great.

(usage) 'That comedian from Cork is a quare head-the-ball.'

Quare fella (n/expr)

An odd or eccentric man.

(usage) 'Yer man paid me double to whip him and then insisted we do penance.'
'Yeah, Cynthia, that bishop's always been a quare fella.'

Rag order (adj)

Unkempt. In disarray.
(usage) 'Me knickers are in rag order.'

Rake (pr)(adj)(v)

A great many.
(usage) 'That gardener's raking in the money!'

Rapid (adj)

Great. Fantastic. Amazing.
(usage) 'Yer mot's knockers are rapid.'

Rarin' to go (expr)

Extremely eager.
Chomping at the
leash.
(usage) 'Maggie's cookin'
was so brutal we were
rarin' to go home.'

Rasher (n)

Slice of bacon (esp.
streaky).
(usage) 'Of course I'm
looking after meself,
Ma. I eat six rasher
sandwiches every night
after me eight pints of
lager.'

Rat-arsed (adj)

Very drunk.
(usage) 'I was so rat-
arsed I ate a spice
burger.'

Rat's arse, not give a (expr)

Not care in the least.
(usage) 'There's too much apathy in this company.'
'I couldn't give a rat's arse.'

Reddner (n)

Blush.
(usage) 'I'll tell ye, Mary, it was so small he had a reddner.'

Redser (n)

A person with red hair.
(usage) 'His mot's a redser with beautiful hair that goes right down her back. Unfortunately she's none on her head.'

Ride (n)(v)

An attractive female or male. To partake in sexual intercourse.
(usage) 'I had a ride off that ride in Accounts.'

Root, to (1) (v)

To search for.
(usage) 'I was having a root for her bra fastener when she gave me a root in the nuts.'

Root, to (2) (v)

To kick forcefully.
(usage) 'He was taking so long to find my bra fastener I gave him a root in the nuts.'

Ructions (n)

Loud verbal commotion.
(usage) 'There were ructions in the County Council when their junket to the Bahamas was cancelled.'

Runner, do a (expr)

Flee. Exit rapidly.
(usage) 'Ah Jaysus, some gurrier did a runner with me Garda car!'

THOSE CHINESE DID A RUNNER
WITH SONIA'S GOLD MEDAL.

Sambo (n)

A sandwich.
(usage) 'You can't beat an egg, bacon, sausage and black pudding sambo for a bit a classy nosh, eh, Taoiseach?'

Sanger (n)

Sandwich.
(usage) 'I'd love to be the meat in a sanger between those two mots.'

Savage (adj)

Great. Tremendous.
*(usage) 'Twelve pints
followed by a large
chips and double batter
burger is absolutely
savage.'*

Scanger (n)

Female lacking in
sophistication.
*(usage) 'The scanger
drank her finger bowl.'*

Scarlet (adj)

Embarrassed. Blushing.
*(usage) 'I was scarlet
when I found out
afterwards that he was
a bishop.'*

JAYSUS, THAT
WAS GREAT!

Scelp (v)

Give a very short haircut.
(usage) 'Jaysus, Trish, see how they scelped ye down below for the operation? It makes ye look years younger!'

Scran (n)

Food.
(usage) 'The fat-arsed cow eats more scran than a horse.'

Scratcher (n)

Bed.
(usage) 'If you're not out of the scratcher and here in ten minutes operating on this man's brain, you're fired.'

|← TIPSY →| |← MERRY →| |←

Scrubber (n)

Woman of low
moral fibre and little
sophistication.
*(usage) 'She's such
a scrubber that she
smokes during oral sex.'*

Scuttered (adj)

Inebriated.
*(usage) 'I was so
scuttered that the
estate agent started to
sound honest.'*

→| |←——— PISSED ——→| |←——SCUTTERED——→|

Scutters (n)

Diarrhoea.
*(usage) 'Eight pints
of Harp and a curry
always gives my missus
the scutters.'*

Session (n)

A prolonged drinking
bout.
*(usage) 'The Cabinet
regularly hold
emergency sessions.'*

Shag (v)

To have sexual
intercourse.
*(usage) 'That Viagra is
great shaggin' stuff.'*

Shaper (n)

Person who walks
with exaggerated strut
to effect 'coolness'.
*(usage) 'He was such
a shaper that when he
walked up to me he gave
me a black eye with the
back of his knee.'*

Shattered (adj)

Very tired. Requiring sleep.
(usage) 'Listen, Taoiseach. The whole Cabinet's been working for nearly an hour and we're all shattered.'

Shenanigans (n)

Mischievous, suspicious, underhand, devious goings-on.
(usage) 'Next item on today's County Council agenda: planning shenanigans. Sorry, uh, planning submissions.'

Shite (adj)

Of extraordinarily poor quality.
(usage) 'The health service is shite.'

Shite hawk (n)

Swine. Pig. Scumbag.
*(usage) 'When I asked
that shite hawk Sean
what we'd use for
protection, he said
we could use de bus
shelter.'*

Shitting bricks (adj)

Extremely fearful.
*(usage) 'I'm shittin'
bricks the doctor'll
tell me I've got acute
diarrhoea.'*

Shower of savages (expr)

Loud, ignorant,
unsophisticated crowd
of people.
*(usage) Q: 'Who's that
shower of savages in
the corner?'*
A: 'That's the Cabinet.'

Sickner (n)

PUKING ON YOUR SHOES IS A SICKNER

Something very upsetting.
(usage) 'Gettin' a dose of the clap from Anto was a real sickner.'

Single (n)

Bag of chips.
(usage) 'Micko was so good in bed I nearly dropped me single.'

Sketch! (expr)

THE ART TEACHER'S COMING! QUICK EVERYONE ... SKETCH!

CLASS 2B

Used in school to indicate approach of a teacher.
(usage) 'Sketch! Quick, Mick, better take yer boot off little Johnny's head.'

Skiver (n)

Person who avoids honest work.
*(usage) Kid: 'When I grow up I want to be a skiver like you, Dad.'
Dad: 'So you want to work in the insurance industry, then?'*

Slag (v)

Make fun of a person in a light-hearted, friendly manner.
(e.g.) 'Yer a big ignorant sleeven of a muck savage, ye thick bogtrotter ye.'

Slapper (n)

Female of low morals and poor taste in clothing.
(usage) 'You're not really going to make that slapper a Minister, are you, Taoiseach?'

Slash (n)(v)

Urination.
*(usage) '... if I may
interrupt my learned
friend, m'Lud, as I'm
dying for a slash.'*

Sleeveen (n)

Devious, sly, repulsive
individual.
*(e.g.) Any member of
Ireland's car insurance
industry.*

Sloshed (adj)

Totally drunk.
*(usage) 'I was so sloshed
I actually believed a
solicitor.'*

Snapper (n)

Baby.
(usage) 'If he wants to have one more snapper I swear I'm going to snap the bleedin' thing off.'

Sound (adj)

Good. Solid. Dependable.
(usage) 'That ventriloquist is a sound fella.'

Spondulicks (n)

Money.
(usage) 'Hee hee, gentlemen. Wait'll ye see the spondulicks our insurance company screwed out of Irish drivers last year.'

Spud (1) (n)

Potato.
(usage) 'She has a head like a raw spud.'

Spud (2) (expr)

Nickname for anyone with the surname Murphy.
(usage) 'Yer man Spud has a head like a raw spud.'

Steamboats (adj)

> Completely intoxicated.
> (usage) 'The two old
> battleships at the bar are
> steamboats.'

Stop the lights! (expr)

> What! I don't believe it!
> (usage) 'A non-corrupt
> planning official? Stop the
> lights!'

Suckin' diesel, now yer (expr)

Now you're talking!
Now you're doing
well!
*(usage) 'Increase car
insurance premiums
by 20% for no reason?
Now yer suckin' diesel,
Mr Chief Executive!'*

Taig (n)

Northern Irish term
for a Catholic.
*(usage) 'The Vatican is
full of Taigs.'*

Teemin' (adj)

Packed.
*(usage) 'The massage
parlour was teemin'
with politicians, priests
and judges, Sarge.'*

Teemin' (v)

Raining heavily.
*(usage) 'It was teemin'
the entire week I was in
the sunny south-east.'*

MORE SUN
CREAM, DEAR?

Thick (adj)

Extremely stupid.
*(e.g.) The person who
conceived RTÉ's 'Angelus'
slot.*

Throw shapes (v)

To swagger excessively. To show off.

(usage) *'Will you stop throwing shapes at those slappers or we'll never get a bleedin' shag.'*

Tip (n)

Messy establishment or room.

(usage) *'The bedroom was a complete tip after the chip fight.'*

Togs (n)

Swimming shorts.
*(usage) 'Jackie's togs
have the same amount
of material as a hanky.'*

Traipse (v)

Walk heavily or
wearily.
*(usage) 'The Irish
team traipsed into the
dressing room after
losing 5-0.'*

Trap (n)

Mouth.
*(usage) 'Ok. Can
everyone on this charity
board keep their trap
shut about rifling the
donations for a junket
to Thailand?'*

Trick-act, to (v)

To mess about, to indulge in horseplay.
(usage) 'I was just trick-acting with Deirdre and hey presto, she's bleedin' pregnant.'

Twist (n)

Round of drinks.
(usage) 'Right. Who's twist is it?'
'Dunno. Everyone's twisted.'

Up the flue (expr)

Pregnant.
*(usage) 'Mick an' me
tried fifty-four times
before I was up the
flue. I'll tell ye, that was
some weekend!'*

Up the pole (expr)

With child. Pregnant.
*(usage) 'Great news, Ma,
I'm up de pole. I mean,
eh, engaged.'*

Wagon (n)

Unattractive female.
*(usage) 'Better gimme
another pint. She still
looks like a wagon.'*

Wear, to (v)

To engage in a
prolonged, passionate
kiss.
*(usage) 'Me an' Anto
just started wearin' and
before I knew it we
weren't wearin' anything.'*

WHAT WILL I WEAR AT
THE PARTY TONIGHT?

ME?

West Brit (n)

Derogatory term
for Irish person who
copies the accent and
mannerisms of a posh
British person.
*(usage) 'This West Brit
asked me for directions.
So I told the fecker to
get a bleedin' life.'*

Wobbler, throw a (expr)

Lose one's temper.
*(usage) 'Me Ma threw
a wobbler just because
I left me dirty jocks on
the kitchen table.'*

Wojus (adj)

Extremely poor quality.

(usage) 'The bus service, the health service, the train service, the telephone service and every other bleedin' Government service in Ireland is wojus.'

Wrecked (adj)

Extremely tired. Worn out.

(usage) Ex-civil servant: 'I'm wrecked doing this ... what d'ye call it?' Private employee: 'Work.'

Yard, get up the (expr)

Get lost!

(usage) 'So, you drank three quarters of it before you realised it was a bad pint? Get up the yard!'

Yer wan (n)

Female whose
name escapes one.
Nondescript individual.
*(usage) 'Yer wan over
there. Yeah, her. Me
wife.'*

Yoke (1) (n)

Any object.
*(usage) 'Anto's got a
lovely yoke.'*

THE DUBLIN
YOKE

Yoke (2) (n)

Derogatory term for
person of uncertain
character (esp.
female).
*(usage) 'The paralytic
one swinging her bra
over her head is a right
yoke.'*

Yonks (n)

A very long time.
(usage) 'It'll be yonks upon yonks before Ireland win the World Cup.'

Youngwan (n)

Female youth.
(usage) 'Hey you, youngfellas, here's youngwans!'

You're wha? (expr)

Alleged method of proposing to one's sweetheart on Dublin's northside.
(usage) 'You're bleedin' wha?'

Zeds (n)

Sleep.
*(usage) 'I caught a few
zeds last night while
Mick was making love
to me.'*

ALSO AVAILABLE

WHO'S FECKIN' WHO IN IRISH HISTORY
20 THINGS TO DO IN DUBLIN BEFORE YOU GO FOR A FECKIN' PINT
WHAT ARE WE FECKIN' LIKE?
THE FECKIN' BOOK OF IRISH LOVE
IN THE NAME OF JAYSUS! STUFF THAT DRIVES IRISH PEOPLE
ROUND THE FECKIN' BEND
THE FECKIN' BOOK OF EVERYTHING IRISH
NOW THAT'S WHAT I CALL A BIG FECKIN' IRISH BOOK
THE BOOK OF FECKIN' IRISH TRIVIA

FOR MORE INFORMATION, VISIT
WWW.OBRIEN.IE/THE-FECKIN-COLLECTION